in case of emergency press

We are proud to acknowledge the Traditional Owners of country throughout Australia and to recognise their continuing connection to land, waters, and culture. We pay our respects to their Elders.

We support recognition, reconciliation, and reparation.

No Bird Lives in my Heart

C.W. Bryan

in case of emergency press
https://icoe.com.au
Travancore, Victoria
Australia

Published by in case of emergency press 2024

Copyright © C.W. Bryan 2024
All rights reserved. Without limiting the rights under copyright reserved above, no part of this publication may be reproduced, stored in or introduced into a database and retrieval system or transmitted in any form or any means (electronic, mechanical, photocopying, recording or otherwise) without the prior written permission of both the owner of copyright and the above publishers.

ISBN: 978-0-6486111-5-8

Cover Photograph: Zdeněk Macháček on Unsplash

Cover design: Ward Nikriph

Acknowledgements

My deepest gratitude to those journals that first published my work.

Grocery Poem, Honey, Aisle 9, For the Boy Who Dropped a Sugar Cookie in the Hy-Vee, and *Sylvia Plath* first published by Version 9 Magazine.

Memento Haibun first published by Third Wednesday.

Swordmaster and *Isabella* first published by Ink in Thirds Magazine.

Heirloom first published by Empyrean Literary Magazine.

The Fate of Winter Moths first published by Deep South Magazine.

Fox Haibun first published by Seventh Quarry Press.

Elegy for Celine, Desire, Please, and *Driving Six Hours Home to an Empty House* first published by Bottlecap Press.

For Sam Kilkenny

*without whom these poems would
never have found their way to the page.*

Table of Contents

Brooklyn 1
For Abby 2
Elegy for Puberty 3
Grocery Poem 6
A Conversation 7
Correspondence 8
Magnum Opus 9
Ice Skating 11
Grief Ghazal 12
Isabella 13
Sylvia Plath 14
Ophelia 15
My Church, An Ikon 16
Aisle 9 17
No Bird Lives In My Heart 18
A Metaphor 20
For the Boy Who Dropped a Sugar Cookie in the Hy-Vee 21
Late December 22
Butterflies 23
Memento Haibun 25
The Planets 26
Marsh View 29
The Heron 30
Getting the Mail 31
Eulogy 32
Wedding Toast 33
Honey 34
Horseshoe 35
Johnston, Iowa September 2, 2023 36
Walking 37
Elegy for Celine 38
Swordmaster 39

Heirloom 40
A Date with Van Gogh 41
The Fate of Winter Moths 42
Fox Haibun 44
For my Father..45
Elegy for a Cat...47
Driving Six Hours Home to an Empty House............................ 48
Desire... 49
Laughter... 50
That's Enough... 51
Please 52
Utopia 53

About the Author **57**

No Bird Lives in my Heart

C.W. Bryan

Brooklyn

Someone else is killing the spiders in your bathroom now.
Not with the palm of a hand, either,
    like I did,
but with the bottom of a dress shoe perhaps

that was left hastily in the hallway, still tied tight as your chest in the moment you see a spider in your bathroom. Or, if you could have it your way, the spider wouldn't die at all despite the laces of a dress shoe that strangle your heart with fear each time they scurry across the white tile floor.

If you could find the courage, or perhaps the right man, the spider would get the happy ending, covered with an empty glass on top of an unpaid water bill. You would carry him, despite the fear, out the window, out that cracked window, onto the fire escape.

For now, however, black guts get stuck in the grout—and they remind you of me. I am black spider guts in the grout of a white tile floor in Prospect Heights.

Better to exist in agony than disappear entirely.

For Abby

Like an old dog
my reflection greets me
at the front door of
every mirror in my house.

It scratches at the fence
of my ribcage. Its howls
echo in my chest.

Our dog Abby died three years
ago. She should have prepared
me for this, but her barks
were full of love, not the
wet cement of expectations.

Elegy for Puberty

1.

I thought it was my spine
snapping, at first that's what
I thought it was, my spine
giving out.

It wasn't though. Cruelly,
it never is.

Such a stupid thing to do,
hiding half a stick of French bread
beneath my pillow. Worse still,
falling asleep naked so, exposed.

I hid the half a stick of French bread
beneath my pillow. I didn't know
what else to do but I couldn't do nothing—
my spine never snapped, or more cruelly

I never understood why I should
want it to. I heard my sister whispering
one night, to her friend, the one I saw changing
in the bathroom earlier that day, she said

it gets hard, it does! and they laughed
and laughed. So I knew it got hard. I saw
her friend changing in the bathroom but I never
even told her my name.

2.

My sister would take out her own trash
all the time. She thought
we wouldn't see what was happening to her vagina.

One night, after dinner, she picked up
the lid of a tomato paste can. It was
smaller than a baseball card.

She picked it up right out of the trash can.
It was so round,
 so red.

She walked over to me.
I was sitting at the counter.
She smelled like iron and cinnamon sticks.
She pressed the tomato paste lid,
it was smaller than a granola bar,
against my arm, right above my elbow
and cut me in one quick motion.

It was so red, the lid was.
I bled right on down past my elbow,
right on down past the little lake of my elbow,
I bled right on down to the floor.

It was warm, the blood, my toes got
sticky as I stepped in it, but I can't
remember the pain, if it ever
existed at all.

3.
Growing up, my sister and I
had to share a bathroom,
which was okay with me.
In our shower, her long
brown hair clung to the whiteness
like wet rats—God, they were so

malleable. I could draw my finger along
the slick-with-steam walls and the rats
would scurry around my finger as if it
were made of peanut butter.

Their bodies would twist around my fingertip
and their bones moved like spaghetti.
When I was naked and clean and new
I would scoop them up, twisting my palms together,

their wet, rat bodies flared with friction, coiling
into tiny brown balls, to sink, lonely,
into the toilet bowl.

Then, I flushed their little rat lives down the drain.
I was king of the world, for a second, I tasted that power.

4.
My sister is dead now.

Deader than rats in a toilet, or
at least as dead.

Her friend is still alive, and I bet
she still changes her clothes all the time,
I bet she doesn't even know my name.

What is the point of it all?
What is the point of

all the bones snapping,
all the blood,
all the trips to the trash can,
all the mornings spent worried she
was dying because of all the blood,
all the laughter—the metallic memory of pain,
all the bones snapping,

if, in the end, she still ended up
lonely as a finger on the wall of a shower,
transient as steam on the wall of a shower,
lifeless as hair on the wall of a shower?

Grocery Poem

A gray and white cat sidles up
        against the splotchy green dumpster
and meows despite himself.

The plastic lid slams hard at the end
of another long shift. It sounds desperately final,
like the North Springs station, or the highest note

of a violin.

A Conversation

I have a six-dollar
fan on the front porch. He
doesn't say much, just
turns his head from left
to right, scanning the summer
evening.

Have you ever seen a thing so stoic?
Has bravery ever been defined so well?

Not since the flag in our
garden, who weathered hail
and rain without complaint, was
crushed by a suicidal tree branch.
I asked the fan if he heard
the flag cry out in pain,
or ripple in fear. He just shakes
his head left, then right, then
left again. I believe him. If
he'd heard, surely he would
have packed it all in and left.

Correspondence

Beneath my feet,
with the sound of a silhouette—
a thrush walking on pinestraw—
light shatters, not like glass,
but like false beliefs.

They splinter in the shape of the whole,
they could be put back together,
       gently,
like a shoveled sidewalk. If only,   anyone
were around to do it.

Magnum Opus

My girlfriend is not a poet in the way
that most people mean. She is a collector
of rare and valuable information. Today,

she told me about cats & the color of their coats.
We adopted a cat recently, a baby thing
with elastic legs & a penchant for biting paper.

She is the color of dust after placing a screw
in the drywall to hang up a favorite painting,
likely a print of Magritte's *Son of Man*.

We call the kitten Tiny Baby. A nickname—an effort
to delay the inevitability that accompanies a name.
My girlfriend told me that Tiny Baby would not

be the color of drywall forever. Her coat
is cold-activated, she said, an abstract form of albinism.
The coldest parts of her body, ones

closest to the grave, will get darker. The kitten
will develop brown gloves on her hands and feet,
a little tuft on the tail, as if that would help hide

the dirt. One foot in the grave and all that.
My girlfriend said that when she gets old, the cat I mean,
her circulation fails & her now warm blood becomes

cool blood becomes slow blood & the cat will be
extremely brown. Here I was, thinking when warm
blood becomes cool blood becomes slow blood

she would be dead. I do not envy her, my girlfriend
I mean, how sweet it must have tasted—the apple.
How rich at first it must seem. Until

one day you realize that each new brown fiber,
each new high-effort hair, isn't brown like an acorn,
or perhaps an open gate, but rather brown like

an apple seed, brown like the required 199 apple seeds
that need to be ingested before a human being dies
from cyanide poisoning (per my girlfriend). I am

a poet, my girlfriend is a collector of knowledge,
Death is a modern artist whose brush stroke falls
in earthen tones on the coat of a kitten.

No doubt his magnum opus.

Ice Skating

At Lake Mission Bell, after the winter scared it solid, kids carve short stories in broken, confused cursive into the ice with pens of sharpened steel. It's a beautiful thing to watch geniuses compose their art. The other night, before the winter sun fell back into the earth and before the ice reclaimed its smooth canvas, I caught a glimpse of the beginnings of a child's magnum opus. I'll do my best to translate the figure eights and cursive Gs or Ys. I'm not a professional but it read something like this:

"My cousin put an Ace of Spades in his bike wheel, and it goes *thwap-thwap-thwap-thwap* (this goes on for a while) and I love the *thwaps* so much I put the Queen of Hearts in mine and now we thwap all over town and down to the mini-mart to buy Gatorade and KitKat bars. There's nothing else I'd rather do and there's no better card than the Queen of Hearts except for maybe the Ace of Spades."

Grief Ghazal

It gets hard-
er to believe
in magic after

your heart shatt-
ers for the first
time. It gets

harder to see pic-
tures through
the filigree of

lattice wood-
work in a confessional
door. I have a friend

who never shiv-
ers in a breeze. I
hope the wind

will frame
her too-familiar
face instead of

fizzling out. Ov-
er my neighbor's
roof the sun still

rises proudly, un-
sure if I live
here anymore.

It gets hard-
er to believe
in magic when
all the lights are out.

Isabella

"It is best to smoke in winter," she said. She opened her pink mouth and let the smoke out very slowly. She was not exhaling, just letting the smoke creep out. It stuck its little white hands out first, pulling itself out of the cavern of her lungs. It ascended like vines. Growing toward the sky, occupying whatever space it could find. Her lungs were probably black with tar, though. They were shrunken lungs. They looked like walnuts. I saw that in a textbook once. It made me want a cigarette. It made me hungry.

"It is best to smoke in winter because you cannot tell what is smoke and what is breath," she said. I thought about this.

"And."

"And nothing. That's it. You just can't tell."

Sylvia Plath

There are grill marks on the frozen chicken
  though they've never known the grill.

The man in line behind me laughs
  and it's warm like orange oven coils.

I miss
  Sylvia Plath

and hate the grill marks on the frozen chicken.

Ophelia

for Colin

You can leave out sunflower seeds
on top of that empty birdbath your
mother bought for you when you moved in.

You can name the squirrels that come
to eat them, things like Ophelia or
Daphne, or any of your other heroines.

You can needle-felt a little witch hat
the size of a thimble to strap on the
head of one of those gluttonous squirrels.

You can see your self reflected in the
blackened, glassy, fear-filled eyes of Ophelia,
so dark and wet you could drown in them.

My Church, An Ikon

for Loo

Five of my friends live together, two couples and a single guy. Four of them are left-handed. What are the odds of that? Slim to none. This is the least fallacious argument for God I can come up with. The right-handed guy, the single one, is a painter. The last piece he made is of a man in a top hat he named Tall Man Gray. He has a basketball in his left hand, a King James bible in his right. It hangs now on my office wall.

Aisle 9

Cracking like a bat,
the summer storm
moves in quick
like ants to aisle nine
where chocolate chips
litter the floor
and the culprit runs away,
scared of the thunder.

No Bird Lives In My Heart

after Charles Bukowski

No bird lives
in my heart. An
inhospitable place, flooding
every morning
with curious
blue blood.

The bird I know
lives
in the park or,
the zoo, or maybe
the splintered telephone poles
on Cherokee.

He does worry after
me. I can
hear him, his corvid
questions, "When
are you quitting cigarettes? When
are you making that
cranberry
and arugula salad?
Did you have that
dream again?"

I used to worry after
him, too. Human
questions like, "Where
do you go in
freezing

rains? Did you ever
know your
grandfather?
Do you ever cry
late at night?"

But,
today I saw him pull
an apple slice
from a torn
plastic bag. Now
I know he's never
shed
a tear in his life.
Just like he knows
that I'll never eat
cranberry
and arugula salad.

We lock eyes in
the park. My heart
pumps blood. Then—
again.

A Metaphor

The bathroom walls in Church Bar are all peeling paint. I am six or seven beers deep. I am staring at the bathroom walls in Church Bar.

When I unfocus my eyes, I can see your face.
That is not to say your face looks like the
bathroom walls in Church Bar. This part is the metaphor—
the part of the poem that allows me to say

I miss you

without having to throw up in front of the bathroom walls in Church Bar. Their paint is peeling, and I am embarrassed by their honesty.

For the Boy Who Dropped a Sugar Cookie in the Hy-Vee

I'm sorry, child
but you cannot escape
the sad trap of gravity.

I'm sorry, child
that you had to learn so early
what sprinkles sound like
as they hit the floor.

Late December

The wind whips my hands as I refill my tires. It is eleven degrees outside. The tips of my fingers turn red. A small man exits the gas station holding a tall styrofoam cup. Coffee steams from the small hole in the lid. He swallows the steam and begins bouncing on the balls of his feet. He is maybe five feet tall. My fingers slip and the stream of air meant for my tires hits me square in the eyeball. The machine lets out a soft beep. I am out of quarters. The small man is bouncing on his heels now, watching me. We are alone in the parking lot. It is near January and the throes of winter are hard on our heels. I begin to bounce on the balls of my feet, and blink until my eyes are wet again.

Butterflies

I knew a girl
once who had
a clothesline that ran
across her kitchen.
When she would water
her houseplants,
she could never remember
how much
water each one needed
to maintain a healthy
green glow.
She said, "I'd rather them
leak than go
thirsty."
She placed neatly folded paper
towels beneath
each green roommate.
An hour after
each over-watering
she would
pick up the paper
towels, whispering
sweet words of encouragement
to each plant.
She would then stand
on a box of cat litter,
hanging each paper towel
up to dry,
from the kitchen
clothesline,
in the yellow, electric light.

I loved her once.
The way those towels
hung, limp, shifting
in the breeze
of drafty doors
reminded me
of butterflies.

Memento Haibun

My grandfather made a gift of his pocketknife. It wasn't in his will or anything, he just quietly took my hand, put the silver knife, shining after all these years, into my palm and folded his wrinkled, work-worn hands around my twelve-year-old fingers. The handle was cool and smooth to the touch. It didn't come with a card; no words were spoken—just the knowing look of a shared secret.

Cutting through
the summer breeze—
single blade of grass

The Planets

after Gustav Holst

Do you remember when you told me that story
of all the Planets in the sky and how they all
had different jobs—different people they
were in charge of?

1.

In the first hour of our road trip, when the first 30
minutes had passed into silence, you said
that Uranus was a magician, and he was friends with
all the squirrels and mice and kindly rodents
of the forest. They would climb on his shoulders
or eat pieces of hard, white cheese out of his wrinkled
hands. You said it was Heaven on Earth to be
a rodent in Uranus's company because as soon
as the cheese ran out, Uranus would open up a little
black book and cast a brand-new dairy-oriented spell.

2.

We had to take our first pit stop 2 hours into the trip
because you hate eating breakfast right when you wake
up and your stomach was starting to interrupt your
stories. The checkout clerk didn't laugh at your 9 a.m.
jokes and didn't even bother to say you're welcome
after your second, emphatic thank you. When you
closed the car door with all your strength you told
me the story of Mars, the bringer of War, and how
he owed you a favor. You would send him in to shake
all the racks of snacks until they fell on the floor,

or to steal all the mustard packets from the roller
grill. I told you that wasn't fair to the other patrons
and you, in your infinite kindness, relented and took
a great big sip of your 64 oz frozen soda-pop.

3.

The road stretched out before us in a long, black
and yellow runway. 64 ozs later we had to stop
again. It was my turn to drive, which meant it was
your turn to play the music. The sun was hiding
behind the clouds like your little niece behind
your sister's skirts at family reunions so you played
a few somber, sullen tunes to mimic the day.
An hour into my driving stint the sun grew more
and more confident, daring to peek around the
cumulonimbus skirt and shed a little light for
our humble journey. The music became joyous,
upbeat yet serene. And you: you became
inspired, telling me that Venus, the bringer
of Peace sent the sun to light our way and break
the melancholy landscape into transcendental
scenes, as she had done for you a million times before.

4.

We were halfway to Iowa and Lethargy was not far
behind us. He had a late start but we all know Lethargy
is a health freak and would never drink 64 oz frozen
soda-pops which means he doesn't have to stop
and pee so often. I was getting nervous because
it seemed every time you blinked it would take
longer and longer for you to open your eyes again.
So you told me about Mercury, the winged Messenger,
and how he was so swift and lithe and angelic.
You were seriously considering cashing in that

favor with the Warbringer because you thought
that maybe you could have asked him to get
Mercury to pick us up and fly right over I-35
traffic all the way through Missouri's unengaging
landscape.

5.

As we finally crossed into Osceola, you introduced
your favorite planet, Neptune. You said he was a
mystic and for half a dollar he could tell me how I
would die and I said that I'd rather save the half
a dollar to buy a gumball and watch the pink
or blue or yellow orb roll down the runway
until it hit the metal door of the dispenser with a clink.
I remember you laughed at that. I remember that your
stories would shrink the miles and the hours down
into manageable parts until the eighteen-hour road trip
ended in Des Moines and you said, exhausted,

6.

Saturn was the bringer of Old Age but you
hypothesized if we stayed in the car and
kept driving that Saturn would just get tired
and leave us alone so we packed up and took
the nearest exit for the Yukon Territory. You
looked beautiful then, basking in Saturn's rage
and you still haven't aged a damn day.

Marsh View

My parents moved recently—
a nice place, marsh view,
plenty of trees and walking trails,
a nice big kitchen for Scottish breakfasts.
Their deck upstairs looks out
on the marsh water shining in the sun.
The aquatic landscape broken only
by the stilted legs of hungry herons.
The floorboards no longer creak
beneath my ochre footsteps
as they once did, in a house filled
with absence, filled with the pink
vernal blossoms of childhood.
I feel like a visitor here—a tourist.
I wonder how much of myself
was left in those creaking planks?
How much of my life is threaded
in their wooden veins?
Perhaps this new deck doesn't creak
only because I've shed the weight
of my childhood, the cloak
of memory—disrobed I am refreshed
like new bamboo shoots in spring.

The Heron

for Danielle

During the peak of low-tide the only water in the marsh resides like a thin film over the surface, as if the whole of it were wrapped in Saran wrap. The thin plastic scene is buffeted on either side by a thin forest. A few gnarled branches reach their ashen hands toward the sky, tugging on the low-hanging skirts of morning fog, each vying for the sun's attention to ask if they might slowly peel off the thin layer of plastic. A heron calls from off-screen. The sound carries itself proudly along the shallow water before tripping and sinking slowly into the mud, where the crabs begin to stretch and stir.

Getting the Mail

Watching someone
you don't know
pick out mail
from your childhood mailbox.

Eulogy

Recently I've been thinking about that eight-foot
plot of land outside of Heathers that my parents
buried my grandfather in. It's amazing how many
tulips and roses can fit in an eight-foot plot of land.
At his funeral my father gave the eulogy and he said
beautiful things, painted him a saint.
It was all true. He was a saint in his own way.
My father said he never once yelled at the dog
for slobbering all over his recently shined shoes
and he gave the mailman lemonade and granola bars.
He said that my sweet grandfather even listened to every
solicitor who came to knock upon his dark red front door.
That story in particular drew a laugh of admiration
and looks of awe. I've never met a man who would listen
to any solicitor at the front door, much less every one.
If I had been old enough at the time to really know
how to give a speech about the dead to a room full
of living people without crying I would have said
that my grandfather was a shepherd, with flocks of
children in his herd that he would lead to ice cream
parlors and apple orchards with the gentle nudge of
a seasoned guide. And God, was he good at it. I bet
that's what he's doing right now: Guiding the children
taken too early to the heavenly ice cream parlor for their
first taste of divine buttered pecan in a fresh-baked waffle cone.

Wedding Toast

I am at a wedding in Iowa.

She called to tell me that the orange afterimage from that afternoon five years ago had filled her brain for the first time in years. I don't have the heart to tell her

I am at a wedding in Iowa

and that the memory of her sits in the front of my mind each day like a scarecrow in a cornfield. It wouldn't break her heart or anything—nothing would, but I can't bring myself to tell her that I have stolen her likeness, I have hired a gardener, someone to tend the apricot trees she planted,

someone to prune the nuptial-white dust from the perennial flowers that grow in her stead.

Each time I pick one, her hips move through the grocery store, her laugh echoes in a vinyl booth,
her hand moves a pawn one square forward. I stick it in the windowsill, right behind my eyelids
and slake my thirst on tepid water.

None of this would break her heart, of course—nothing would.

I don't tell her about the wedding, the one in Iowa, just in case.

Honey

Honey is the only animal product
that remains non-perishable.
It never curdles or rots—
honey lives forever.

When I was a child
my friends and I would kill
bees with tennis rackets.
I didn't know yet, about the honey.

Horseshoe

You must not be sleeping well either. Midnight lifts her skirts, dragging sleep along the too-tall grass of my memory. You are there, hair burning in sudden moonlight—wait! Don't run, not again, I do not know how to tend the horses myself. You said three scoops of oats to one part water, but the smell of sweat, and the stillness of white breath clouds my vision. I do not know where you placed the water. It must be scared, in the dark, it must think you are leaving again. Or maybe it remembers what it used to be like, to be held in your hands. A crook of ivory peaks behind the darkness leading the way, but as I reach for your hand, I am left alone, in a stable full of hungry horses. I would be surprised if I ever sleep well again.

Johnston, Iowa September 2, 2023

for Sarah

I think about the water leaking from the ugly popcorn ceiling of our hotel room in Johnston, Iowa and cannot help but laugh.

The water wasn't brown, like a mourning dove, nor malicious, like a funeral dirge—it was just
     water,
that didn't know where else to go. I think about the paint on the roundabouts right off I-35, how maladroitly it clung to cracked pavement, think about its dreams of being on a canvas hanging in the Frick, the feeling of confused drivers running their burning tread over its body,
     instead.

And so these words sit on this page, and I can't bring myself to think where else they would rather be, so I don't. I just place them there, and hope that you can navigate them a little better than the water leaking from the ugly popcorn ceiling of our hotel room in Johnston, Iowa.

Walking

and
in the moonlight there
without you

the world becomes too beautiful to bear.

Elegy for Celine

A soul escaped through no-longer-twitching ears,
not solid like wood chips in a flowerpot—

viscous, ephemeral, dissipating fog
that doesn't rise on its haunches
and move across the harbor.

It slips through my fingers as I try
to shove it in my chest,
push it through my ribcage
wrap my heart around it

eager, anxious

I try to breathe it in, to preserve it somewhere,
anywhere but the brown loops of a dirty shag carpet
where a too-small, too-soon body
lies behind the threshold of a creaking door.

The fog never stays, nor does it rise on haunches.
      I know that now.
I know Carl Sandburg for a liar.

He could never understand
how cold it is, how quiet,
to feel her soul pass through your fingers.

Swordmaster

for Christie

I was the age when your parents give you and your siblings all the same haircut. The same age when you first discover the joy of smashing dandelions, a formative time for any child. I preferred clapping my hands around each flower, prying my sweaty palms apart, slow as a secret, to reveal each white stalk I caught. My sister, however, with our bowl-cut bangs shifting with effort, preferred the stick. She was a swordmaster, a force with dead branches, a miracle to me. In a matter of seconds, twenty dandelions decapitated with eight-year-old grace. Their lithe, skinny green bodies fell to the earth as their soft skulls filled the air like snow on a summer afternoon.

Heirloom

Your mother's glass. The only one in the cabinet that
does not match the others. It's beautiful. Purple

crystal scattered on linoleum like a layer of fine
mauve dust. The first tear falls from a thousand

fractured faces, glistening in the sun. Birds turn
dirges in the late autumn air, as you push slivers

into the dustpan—the vision of her soft hand around
the glass fades with each reluctant sweep. Tears

pool in your eyes and you wonder why she gave you
such maladroit arms, sun-spotted and shaky. Or

a brain wired to prefer the taste of Diet Coke in a
glass over ice, just as your mother did. Shards clink

in the trash, your tears race them to the bottom. The
lid closes in a soft thud—the birds stop singing.

A Date with Van Gogh

Her voice sounds like she's speaking through a fan when she whispers.
She always whispers when we stroll through the colossal Tate.

She's cautious and quiet in case the art may be eavesdropping.
She does the same thing at cemeteries too. The dead don't have much

else to do but listen. Either way, it all seems silly to me, Van Gogh
had a hard enough time hearing when he was alive.

Hedging my bets, I say, "I bet I could have painted that sunflower"
just in case Vincent's good ear is listening in.

"I bet I could kick your ass," he whispers back,
with a voice so tired, like he's heard this all before.

The Fate of Winter Moths

Sitting on the stoop,
concrete sodden with
the chill of late
winter, the air
acquires a coolness
like your first breath
after confessional.
The christmas lights
illuminate the porch
in a motley of whites
and oranges. The
tangerine glow casting
warmth while the sun
is taking his smoke
break. Two sounds
permeate the crisp air
swimming up to my ears
like a swan through
inky lake water:
the languid boughs
sighing in the wind,
scraping their emaciated
limbs together in
contemplation and the
fatal buzz of my
neighbor's bug zapper.
It stands watch like
a plum King's Guard,
never resting in his duty;
an amethyst firebrand.
The absence of the

mosquito's persistent drone
is chilling, and its deafening
vacancy amplifies the
cruel cut of the bug zapper.
In this quiet cacophony
I think that letting moths
fall prey to an
undeserved, mauve, electric
death is the cruelest
thing I've ever known.
I creep back up the
steps and cast a wary
look into my neighbor's
grimy window and am
shocked to see them
sleeping peacefully.

Fox Haibun

If I search through old memories, shaking dust from visions long filed away, I can see scenes from my childhood. Whenever I am feeling old, I pull a few out, polish them up, put them in a frame for a while—constant rotation of nostalgia. They hang on the walls of my skull, eight by eleven inches of glass reflecting the early morning sunlight that pours through my ears.

The vision that hangs behind my forehead now shows me a scene of green and orange on a field of sandy, shell-shocked earth. The fox lived in that great floral house long before we moved in. From our deck, its joints creaking with each small step I took, I watched him check off things from his to-do list—grocery shopping, security checks, singing lullabies and other sweet songs to his children. We weren't friendly neighbors per se, I never learned his name, but we coexisted well enough. From certain angles, he would look up through slatted wood and chitter an amicable 'hello' as he walked off in search of breakfast.

Summer sunrise
behind evergreen curtains—
the fox

For my Father

When I think of my father my heart
starts beating in time with his seven a.m.
footsteps on hardwood floors.
His image rests in the second chamber

of my heart. If I could shrink you
down and put you in there, you'd hear
the sharp, industrial *twang* of golfballs,
scenes of windblown, sun-wrecked dune reeds and shark

fins cresting the ocean's ceiling.
My nose fills with scents of SPF four
and scheduled coffee. Salt spray off
the foreshore permeates the air as he runs

up and down the neural pathways he forged
with white hot affirmations and ice-cold habits.
If you were to run the needle over my
inherited though painted skin, the music would

radiate in clouds of bookstore doorbells,
deafening sneezes and sports bar televisions.
This year I'm starting construction on a new
chamber in my heart: one just to hold

the memories of my father, a chamber filled
with the loud, consistent banging of beanbags on wood,
a chamber big enough for me to chase after
frisbees tossed with sixty-eight-year-old skill.

Most crucially, a chamber with integrity
enough to hold the blue, persistent flame
in focus long enough for me to light my own
cigarette, and smile as the smoke comes out.

The new room design has soundproof walls
and the door and locks are all fireproof,
withstanding flames as hot as the water my
mother uses to wash the greasy meatloaf pans.

Elegy for a Cat

One gentle paw
quiet
as a snowy alley
alights like a dove
on a gray couch

kneading
kneading
kneading
kneading
kneading
kneading
kneading
kneading
kneading
kneading
kneading
kneading
kneading

until she's not.

Driving Six Hours Home to an Empty House

For two-hundred-eighty-four miles continue straight
on I-20 west
but,
life is rarely straight for two-hundred-eighty-four miles.

It is perp
endicular
as a cross
on the side of the highway

      fragile as a wind-whipped ribbon, stained with sunlight,
frayed by longing

sudden twisted metal, bends—
      jagged as a Wednesday evening with a broken guard rail.

It is, life is, this is, waves, a drop
              in the pond

a familiar doorbell chiming in your ears
      two-hundred-eighty-four miles   later.

Even the greener grass that steals my   breath
and marks the graves of men
waves
in a quiet wind.

Desire

I understand it now—
the pinprick

to the side of the thigh.

The sunlight unaware,
one day

after.

The wind, persistent, drying tears
on your face

from an iron park bench
before they can stain your lips

or burn into your skin.

A pin prick to the side of the thigh—
an empty flower pot, once filled with snow.

Laughter

I laughed recently.
　It felt

like opening a letter, seeing your name
scrawled out in a familiar hand,
and the words that follow just say

I'm sorry.

That's Enough

I'd walk again through icy rain to eat a chicken salad sandwich on the world's driest bread with you just one more time. I'd pretend to like seafood and say all the right things like, "shrimp are the blue-collar workers of the ocean and it feels bad to eat them but this cocktail sauce is way too good" and stuff my face.

I'd support everything you say no questions asked even if you do get a tiny bit conspiratorial after the third glass of the house red. I'd tear down those reality TV show posters they hung up on Boulevard which cover your favorite piece of graffiti.

I'd cook you dinner and buy all your favorite ingredients from the grocery store like watermelon radishes and dinosaur kale and all the other vegetables that sound crazy like that. I'd watch all those shark documentaries you love and the more I think about it the more I think I'd punch a shark in the nose, saddle him up and take off for Lisbon where you are right now and say to you,

"I hate shrimp and watermelon radish and red wine and graffiti and I especially hate dry bread
but I love you and I think
                                that's enough."

Please

Beyond   all that
Beyond   bridges

a flower blooms pink first
and   then,
wrapped in snow.

Wrapped in snow, it wilts
with honesty.

Beyond

it   all beyond beyond beyond,

there is a silhouette I can see.
A monolith

wrapped in snow.

Utopia

In the jaws of a dog
        the sanctity of man's best ideas
        are torn up with indifference.
        Life is no way to treat an animal.

About the Author

C.W. Bryan is the author of one previous poetry collection, a chapbook titled **Celine: An Elegy**. He is also the co-founder of *Poetry is Pretentious*, a poetry and arts collective in Atlanta, Georgia, USA. *Poetry is Pretentious* hosts poetry and musical events and publishes small zines and pamphlets by local authors.

Bryan writes poetry, short stories, and creative nonfiction at poetryispretentious.com with his writing partner, Sam Kilkenny.

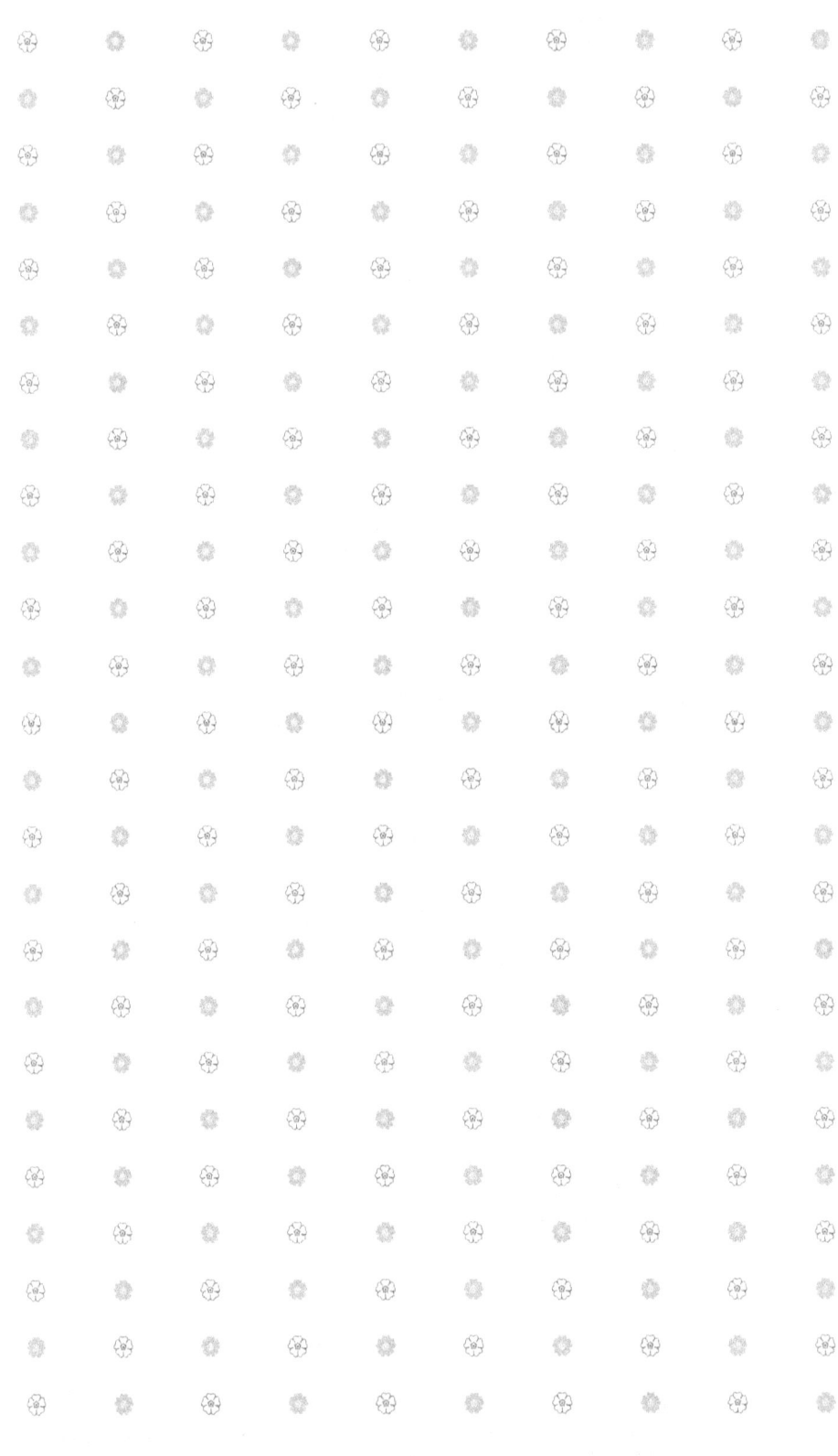

www.ingramcontent.com/pod-product-compliance
Lightning Source LLC
Chambersburg PA
CBHW032016290426
44109CB00013B/685